INK AND EMOTIONS

THE POETRY OF EXISTENCE

BHANNU ARORA

In every special moment's glow,

A poem's magic starts to flow.

My hidden words, once asleep in bed,

Now dance alive, in thoughts widespread.

Contents

Contents

1. Doubt's Shadow

In the world of love, doubt's a sneaky guest,
It makes things messy, puts love to the test.
It pulls us apart, makes trust fade away,
Turns sunny love days into ones that are grey

But remember, doubts are like passing clouds,
Don't let them get loud, or make love feel cowed.
Look into eyes, see the love that's true,
Trust in the heart that beats just for you.

Monarchs grand, in regal attire,
When touched by doubt's ghostly fire,
Saw empires crumble, destinies shift,
As wisdom fled, leaving a rift.

Amidst the fog, let your voice rise,
Unmask the truths, dispel the lies.
In clarity's hold, you'll see,
The unmatched strength of authenticity.

Avoid the trap of doubt, hold love tight,
With trust and understanding, everything will be right.

2. Rising Beyond Anger's Storm

Angers like a bullet, shot on tough days.
Regret follows, setting life ablaze.

In that moment, control you could've held,
Guilt lingers long, but your soul can be swelled.

Use humour to mend the past's strain,
Future awaits, your power to regain.

When anger takes hold, shut your eyes tight,
Pray and smile, with calm, make things right.

3. Companions in the Cosmos

In a world where stars dimly shine,
Moonlight's glow seems less than fine.
Forests sing tales old and profound,
Yet the rhythm of unity, they've rarely found.

Across vast heavens and deep cosmic seas,
Hearts float alone, craving for life's keys.
Towering mountains touch heavens so high,
But in their solitude, they sigh a lone cry.

Bright auroras light up the night's face,
Yet miss the beauty of a shared grace.
The vast universe, in its silent might,
Echoes a truth: alone, things aren't right.

Stars in the sky seek a partner's glow,
Comets wish for mates as they go.
In the cosmic dance, wide and far,
Loneliness is an out-of-tune guitar.

As galaxies meet and stars find their pair,
So should souls end their solitary despair.
For amidst the vastness and stellar light,
With companionship, everything feels right.

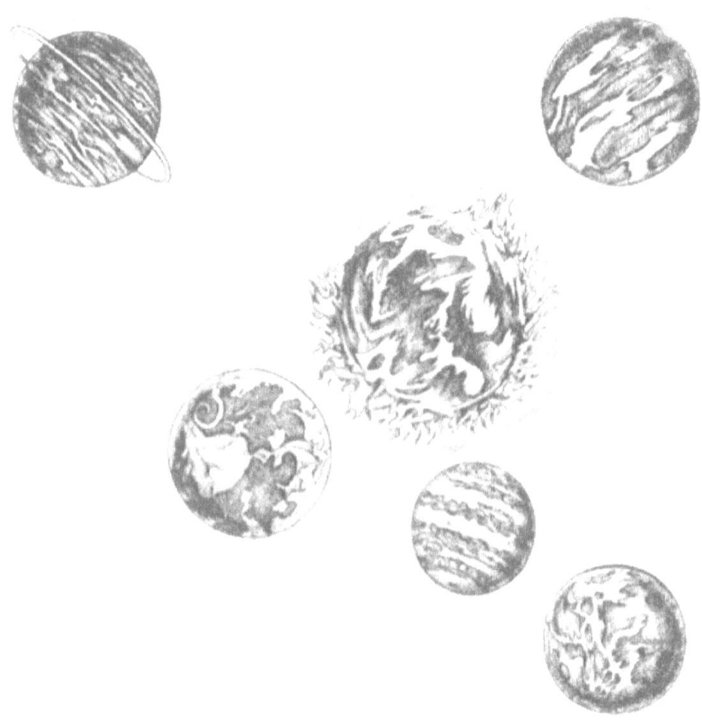

4. The Fall of Pride

I show my pride, always strong.
No questions, no doubts from the throng.
I only want to hear praise,
Believing I do no wrong.

I aim for perfection, every day,
Rising high, not caring what others say.
But I forgot, what rises can fall,
And my pride led me astray.

I woke up alone, my glory gone,
Realized humility is the real dawn.
On Earth, neither heaven nor hell is the key,
It's grounding pride, and then I'll truly be free.

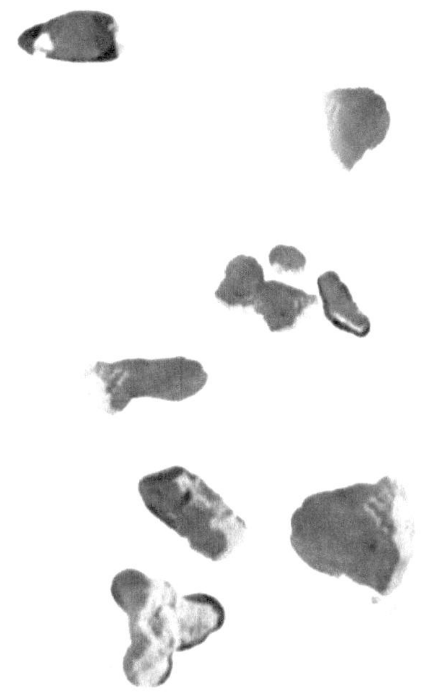

5. Unheard Wishes

I've asked, but often felt unheard,
For health, joy, and a few rewards.
God, why does it take so long?
Where can I go when hopes go wrong?

They say it's all God's plan,
That someday, I'll understand.
But I feel lost and question why,
Why can't life be simplified?

I wished for answers, clear and bright,
Yet God seemed silent, out of sight.
Then a moment came, a shift in view,
I saw blessings, old and new.

I realized I have so much,
And for that, I'm deeply touched.
Life's precious, I won't delay,
I'll cherish every single day.

6. Unwanted Touch

In the quiet corners of your heart,
Whispers emerge, setting you apart.
When an unwanted touch clouds your day,
Remember those whispers, don't let them sway.

Stand with courage, like an age-old tree,
Let your voice rise, firm and free.
Break away from what doesn't feel right,
For your inner compass will guide you to light.

At times, confusion might blur your sight,
And reactions might not take immediate flight.
It's okay to feel lost, it's okay to pause,
But remember, you're your own best cause.

Equip yourself with knowledge and care,
So, the next time you feel that unwarranted glare,
You'll be prepared, strong and true,
To confront the challenge, and see it through.

In every moment, your strength is reborn,

Radiate your essence, let your true self adorn

7. The Dance of Jealousy

Jealousy, with its cunning sway,
Was never your destined path or play.
A lurking spectre, it waits in the corner, so sly,
Ready to pull you down, make your spirits fly awry.

It isn't a comrade, nor a confidant to trust,
But a treacherous tide that can leave hopes in the dust.
Deep is the chasm it digs, dark and steep,
Pushing you to the edge, making the soul weep.

Yet, there's strength within, waiting to be unleashed,
Bid jealousy farewell, let the chains be released.
Move forward, with grace, leaving envy behind,
For in letting go, peace and clarity you'll find.

Tend to your heart, nurture feelings so rare,
Shift from the green shadows, breathe the fresh air.
In the realm where love reigns, pure and true,
Without jealousy's haze, life takes on a vibrant hue.

God's gentle touch, a light in the night,
Guides you away from envy, towards the warm brightness.
In this sanctuary, where love and kindness stand,
You find solace, feeling the divine's soothing hand.

• 13 •

8. Emerging from Shame's Eclipse

In shadows of hurt and lingering doubts,
Self-worth crumbled, echoes of silent shouts.
Lost in a maze, a reflection unknown,
Each corner echoing a sorrowful tone.

Patiently searching for light to break free,
Feeling so small, like a lone leaf on a tree.
The devil's cruel grin, a haunting affair,
Marking the soul with a weight hard to bear.

But from distant horizons, a voice did say,
"Mistakes are human, they've been made by all, every day.
You're not alone in this vast, winding maze,
Find strength, stand tall, and set your spirit ablaze."

Time is a healer, with stories to share,
Forgive yourself, let go of despair.
Facing challenges head-on, with a renewed flair,
Shame diminishes when courage is in the air.

9. No More Silence: Facing Bullying Head-On

In shadows of doubt, my spirit felt confined,

A weight pressing down, mixed feelings intertwined.

My soul cried out, a silent, piercing chime,

Echoing, "You're being bullied, and you're on the line."

With eyes wide, I surveyed the scene,

Invisible figures, their intentions unseen.

Every corner, every whisper, a constant test,

I knew I had to address this unwanted guest.

Friends, peers, and superiors alike,

Their words and actions, sharp as a spike,

Eroding my joy, my essence, my core,

Leaving behind a heart that felt sore.

In turmoil, I pleaded for divine aid,

To escape this storm, this relentless raid.

My joy, my trust, all felt amiss,

Desperately seeking a moment of bliss.

Yet, in silence, a realization did unfold,

My inner strength, fierce and bold.

Challenges faced, I began to see,

The power I held was the key to be free.

When jests about my weight came to play,
I declared, "I am perfect in every way!"
Commands from above, dictating my fate,
I decided, "On my terms, I'll create."

To a young one, facing bullies and their jeer,
I advised, "Speak out, let them hear.
Tell your guardians, your mentors, stand tall,
Together we rise, ensuring bullies fall."

For it's in our will, our unyielding grit,
That we find the path, the strength to commit.
Face these challenges, rise above the abyss,
And in doing so, find life's truest bliss.

10. Wealth

Hey, wealth?
Life seems tethered to your sway.
Even for basic joys and peace,
It's through you, they say.

The more I have, the more I crave,
When scarce, worries do reside.
With more within grasp, ambition grows,
Seeking societal pride and wide.

Yet I paused, stepped back in time,
Shedding all that was just for show.
Within months, sans my luxury ride,
A regal life began to glow.

Dear wealth, it's not you to blame,
It was my heart, lost and confined.
You were meant for essential needs,
Yet I was misled, to you I was blind.

11. In every whisper and rustle, I sense the presence of God

A soft wind's touch,
Trees and skies, so much.
Birdsongs at dawn,
Night and day, life goes on.

Seasons change, colours blend,
Lakes reflect, seas without end.
In heartbeats and quiet peace,
Nature's gifts never cease.

A child's laugh, pure and true,
Flowers bloom in every hue.
Life's simple joys, paths we take,
Nature's wonders, with each step we make.

Creatures many, skies that rain,
Trains and planes, life's busy lane.
Nature's power, its gentle song,
In all of this, we belong.

In these simple things, so clear,
I've found the Divine, near and dear.
Cherish each moment, let love shine,
In every corner, the Divine's sign.

12. The Day the Diary Skipped

Lazing on a chair, in silent peace,
Beneath the vast shelter of a Banyan tree.
A cuckoo's song fills the calm air,
A melody, tender and rare.

Whispers of wind, nature's hug,
The bird's joy, evident in her grace.
Time flowed, yet stood still somehow,
Captured in that singular, endless now.

Sorrows of past began to wane,
Invited her closer, free from pain.
She gleamed, echoing joy so fine,
Together, like two faces of a single line.

She shared tales, her joys and glee,
Night arrived, spanning a timeless spree.
I yearned to pen down the day's song,
Yet, some feelings just don't belong on paper long.

An untouched page might catch your eye,
But know, that day held the sky.
For within my heart, that memory did nest,
A moment heavenly, at its very best.

13. The Mosaic of Peace

In the vast realm where thoughts intertwine,
The quest for peace of mind does shine.
More precious than jewels or gilded gold,
Its value, profound, never gets old.

The clutter of worries, the weight of the night,
Are but fleeting shadows, devoid of true might.
For in the stillness, where silence does reside,
Lies the serene depth, where peace does hide.

Imagine the life, as free as the doves,
Soaring above with no fetters or gloves.
Beyond cages of doubt, past barriers of fear,
In open blue yonder, where vision is clear.

Recall the innocence of a child's gleeful spree,
Or lovers lost in moments, as boundless as the sea.
Life's journey, a mosaic of dreams and songs,
Guiding us gently, where true healing belongs.

The river's gentle murmur, the mountain's old rhyme,

Whisper the secrets of peace, transcending time.
So let go of troubles, welcome the divine dance,
For in the heart's quiet, lies life's truest expanse.

14. Rising Beyond Despair

In the depths of despair,
Where shadows loom large,
You feel adrift,
Like a boat without a barge.

The world seems cold,
Joy, a distant sun.
Laughter fades,
Feels like the end has begun.

Yet, remember this truth,
Older than any lore:
The darkest nights
Often precede the dawn's core.

Take a moment to reflect,
Find peace in the world's vast design,
For amidst life's intricate landscape,
You'll find patches that brightly shine.

For beyond every trial,
Beyond the steepest hill,
Lies strength renewed,
And a spirit that's still.

15. Echoes of Women's Worth

In the fabric of night, vast and deep,
Where dreams are sown and secrets keep,
There lies a tale, ancient and profound,
Of a woman's spirit, unbound.

Every star, a glint of her story,
Every nebula, a fold of her glory,
She's the whisper of winds, the tide's gentle pull,
The fire in the dawn, the night's gentle lull.

Each woman, a chapter, a verse, a line,
Bound by threads of time's design,
From ancestral roots to futures unseen,
She's the keeper of memories, in between.

Mountains stand tall, yet even they know,
The strength of her will, the depth of her woe,
Oceans vast, with mysteries concealed,
Yet in her eyes, all truths are revealed.

To belittle her journey or mock her way,
Is like shunning the sun, casting away the day,
Her resilience, her grace, her undying flame,
Deserve respect, beyond just a name.

For every challenge she overcomes with grace,
For every tear, every smile on her face,
Honour her story, her undying stance,
For she is the rhythm, the music, the dance.

16. Father's Faith

Once in my youth,
High school had me cornered,
Before the Principal's truth,
I stood, my confidence ordered.

Father, a soldier of distant lands,
Guarded borders, heart so grand,
While I, sheltered by grandmother's hands,
Felt lost, in life's shifting sands.

The Principal's voice, stern and loud,
Proclaimed another year, amidst the crowd,
Tears streamed, my pleas in vain,
Inside, I was consumed by pain.

From the shadows, a voice arose,
Steady as the mountain, it confidently shows,
Not God, but my father stood tall,
Defending his son, ensuring I wouldn't fall.

"Let him pass," Father spoke with a tone,
"Another school awaits, where he'll be known.
Not every journey follows the charted course,
Sometimes, one must find their own source."

Grateful, I held the pass in hand,
In a new school, a chance to expand,
I pondered - Father or God, who stands tall?
In that moment, Dad surpassed them all.

Years passed, he never spoke of that day,
Silently understanding, leading the way,
Perhaps he saw my inner strife,
His faith set the course of my life.

For I am who I've become,
Thanks to a father, second to none,
In his eyes, I found my way,
His silent faith, my guide every day.

(A Tale of Truth)

17. Love's Faded Portrait

Once, my heart was captured, true,
By a maiden fair, with eyes so blue.
It felt predestined, like fate's decree,
If she were to wed, it must be with me.

Our circle of friends would gather close,
Where laughter flowed, and tales arose.
Yet, none discerned my hidden desire,
Or the silent storm, my heart's wild fire.

No need for alarms, for each dawn brought cheer,
To the dairy I'd go, hoping she'd appear.
A simple greeting, our shared routine,
Her bright smile, her pup, the perfect scene.

Though just a year apart in age we stood,
My feelings deep, if only she understood.
Then, she shared news of her journey afar,
With her father, like a shooting star.

Days turned gloomy, her absence like a void,
No more the playful pup, mornings devoid.
Then, like magic, she returned one morn,
At the dairy, her presence reborn.

Buying our milk, she offered a stroll,
Dream or reality, my heart on a roll.
Words flowed easily, like a bubbling brook,
Yet, in her narrative, a sudden hook.

She spoke of Harry, joy in her voice,
I inquired, only to face a stark choice.
Her husband, she revealed, casting a gaze,
Understanding the end of my dreamy days.

Our parting felt heavy, laden with unspoken words,
The spilt milk symbolic, of crumbled worlds.
I saw her no more, pain hard to defy,
In sorrow's grasp, I wished to lie.

But time, the healer, carried me through,
To brighter horizons, to vistas new.

18. In the Land Beyond Worry's Hold

In a realm where trees converse and shadows dance,
Worry was a puppeteer, leading minds a merry prance.
Yet, below the velvet sky and above the whispering grass,
Lay secrets to unchain souls, to let the fretting pass.

Worry, the weaver, spun webs of gossamer doubt,
Tales of "what ifs" and "maybes" echoed all about.
Yet the wise old moon, with its luminous sheen,
Whispered tales of release, seldom heard or seen.

"Grasp the moment," it hummed, "with both your hands,
Dance with the present, to life's shifting sands.
For tomorrow's yarn is yet unspun,
Why let today, under weight of worry, come undone?"

The wind, a playful sprite, carried laughter in its sweep,
"Chase me," it teased, "And let your troubles sleep.
In movement, find solace; in action, find your song,
For worry fades when you realize you belong."

The river, with its endless twist and turn,
Told stories of obstacles, of lessons to learn.
"Flow with grace," it murmured, "despite the stone or tree,
See obstacles not as barriers, but paths to be free."

So, in this magical land where nature spoke clear,
The antidote to worry was hope, action, and cheer.
For when we release the now, the present, the bit,
Worries dissolve, and our spirits are lit

19. Action's Anthem

"If he lends a hand,"
"If they stand beside this stand,"
"If her love holds true,"
"If wealth, like seas, flowed through,"
"If he drifts away like sand,"
"If dreams meet reality, oh so grand,"
Endless "ifs," like stars, expand.

Shed the cloak of 'if' with haste,
For you pen life's script, its taste.
Trust in your power, take the throne,
For every step and choice, you own.

Yet, often we pause, never to rise,
While action-borne souls claim the prize.
Mere thoughts usher silent goodbyes,
In a world where movement ties.

Countless visions, yet feet stand still,
Acknowledge the truth, bend to its will.
In action, witness the universe's reflection,
A dance with attraction's affection.

With action, we soar to boundless sights,
Chasing away those restless, endless nights.

20. Missteps, Memories, and Friends

In the company of friends, my spirit takes flight,
A sanctuary where gloom turns bright.
Not just gains, but shared stories that mend,
Such is the magic of a true friend.

Clock hands blur, hours feel like minutes passed,
With genuine pals, joy unsurprisingly lasts.
No pretence, no facades, just hearts that blend,
Real friends stand by you, they won't let you bend.

Recall that night, in our youthful school days,
When a friend thought he'd found the academic maze.
A cheat sheet he provided, thinking we'd soar,
Yet dawn found us cramming, hoping to score more.

But fate, she's a trickster, as we soon found out,
The paper was different, leading to self-doubt.
I was mad, felt betrayed, emotions began to stir,
Thought of calling him foe, not the friend he once were.

But days turned to laughter, as he made me see,
We were both in that mess, as thick as thieves could be.
It's these tales, these blunders, that in time we'd relish,
For friendship's essence, is what makes life flourish.

In the circle of such kinship, our souls truly thrive,
For with true friends by our side, we can but dive.
Into life's many adventures, come rain or shine,
For in their presence, every challenge feels benign

21. Hush of Unspoken Desires.

There she was, a sight so fair,
Lost in dreams, without a care.
Her image haunted every thought,
Sleep escaped, work was for naught.

Heart raced fast, feelings grew,
Wanting her, but what to do?
Love surrounded, filled the air,
But fear held back, it wasn't fair.

Wishing she'd see, hoping she'd know,
Yet courage to approach was slow.
Thoughts spun, "Am I enough?"
Love's path can be so tough.

In the end, here's what I found:
Open your heart, let love resound.
For in taking that chance, bold and true,
Love might just come back to you.

22. Shimla's Snow: A Journey Back in Time

In the heart of Shimla, where hills stand tall,
Mid-aged in spirit, I witnessed my first snowfall.
The world I knew, painted in monochrome shades,
Suddenly burst into white, as sunlight fades.

Each flake descended, a gentle, cold touch,
A sensation so new, it meant so much.
The trees donned a cloak, pristine and white,
The city transformed, in the quiet of night.

As snowflakes danced, on the breeze so slight,
The streets shimmered, under the moonlight.
Though years had passed, with memories long,
In that snowy scene, I felt youthfully strong.

Thrills ran deep, as my steps made a sound,
Crunching and sinking, in the snow-covered ground.
Each moment felt like a childhood's glee,
For the snow in Shimla, had set my spirit free.

Laughter echoed, children and elders alike,
Snowball fights, sleds, and snowman's hike.
For a time, age was but a number, so small,
In the magic of snow, we were young, one and all.

In the heart of winter, as life swiftly flew,
Snow brought a moment, both calming and new.
Though years had layered, and tales had been sung,
That Shimla snowfall made me feel fresh and young.

23. For a Brief Moment

Time seems to race, unyielding, ever swift,
Seeking solace, my spirit needs a lift.
Can the world pause, even briefly in its spin,
To let my weary soul find peace within?

Each dawn brings more of the same,
Yet I yearn for a break from this game.
Illuminate my days, Divine,
In this monotony, let a sign of hope shine.

A hint of joy, a fleeting glee,
A reminder of all I can be.
Just for a moment, guide me, Stars,
Lead me past these worldly scars.

To a realm of dreams, where I can be vast,
Away from the shadows the world has cast.
Crafting my sanctuary, a haven so true,
Where time slows, and life feels brand new.

With every heartbeat, with every sigh,
Let me find answers to the 'why'.
For in this brief moment of clarity and grace,
I'll find strength to continue the race.

24. Breaking Debt's Chains

When debts tower high, casting shadows long,
And every choice you make seems wrong.
When kin and friends, and banks shut doors,
And hope feels distant on distant shores.

Stay steady, my friend, hold your ground,
For in this storm, a way can be found.
No need for distress, no need for haste,
With patience and poise, no effort is waste.

Speak, don't hide, to those you owe,
Your earnest attempts will surely show.
For debts that arise from fate's cruel hand,
Most will understand, where you stand.

Do not let despair take its toll,
Or thoughts so dark, consume your soul.
You are more than the sum of your dues,
Your worth isn't something society gets to choose.

Avoid spiralling deeper into the debt pit,
Address each one, bit by bit.
Consider new ventures, or a different site,
Such changes could set your course right.

Welcome new strategies, follow your heart,

In passion, you might find a fresh start.

Many paths lay hidden in plain view,

Forge ahead, and they'll come into view.

• 45 •

Fear not the whispers, the murmurs, the jests,

Transient are these financial tests.

For when you rise, having faced this test,

They'll seek your counsel, impressed by your quest.

"Nothing's Impossible", more than just words,

It's the anthem of fighters, not just for the birds.

Solutions abound, just look around,

In unexpected corners, answers are found.

Act, don't ponder, seize the day,

For action paves the most potent way.

With the universe as your guiding force,

Soon, life will find its joyful course.

25. Tales of Unfulfilled Dreams

In a land where shadows taste of honeyed lies,
And the silent murmur of unspoken sighs,
There danced a flame with a sapphire hue,
A fire born from wishes never to come true.

The moon whispered secrets to a fish with wings,
Dreaming of stars and golden string.
But in its heart, a yearning so deep,
For oceans vast, where lost dreams weep.

A tree with feathers tried to soar,
Beyond the clouds, to lands of yore.
Yet roots of longing held it tight,
Anchored to memories, day and night.

In the alley of dreams where time does bend,
Unfulfilled desires, their letters send.
Each one sealed with a tear and a jest,
"To the universe," they plead, "grant our request."

But sometimes magic lies in the chase,
In the journey, not the hold.
For in the art of seeking what's afar,
We find beauty, right where we are.

26. Lost and Found

• 47 •

In the garden where two hearts dwell,
Sometimes secrets can start to swell.
Drawn to another, though vows were said,
Walking on paths where few dare tread.

Why does it happen? Why go astray?
Maybe love's light has dimmed some way.
Or a need to feel valued, seen and heard,
Pushes one toward a different word.

But an affair, though tempting it seems,
Is not a solution, nor answers dreams.

To handle this challenge, look deep inside,
Open up, talk, no secrets to hide.

Seek understanding, not just the blame,
Remember the start, the initial flame.
To step back from the edge, to find the door,
One must cherish the love, felt before.

An affair's a sign, a wake-up, a nudge,
It's not the end, but one shouldn't fudge.
To heal and to grow, be true and be clear,
Choose love and trust, over secrets and fear.

27. Lifted Spirits

In every sunrise, a promise is born,
To face each day, to greet the morn.
For happiness isn't a fleeting prize,
But a choice we make under the skies.

Life has its ups, and its downs too,
Yet joy is a lens, a brighter view.
Even in storms, when clouds are Gray,
A cheerful heart finds a brighter way.

Being happy, isn't just for you,
It spreads around, and lifts others too.

Like ripples in water, your joy will spread,
Touching all in its path, wherever it's led.

So choose to be cheerful, come what may,
Light up your world, chase gloom away.
For happiness is more than a feeling inside,
It's a beacon of hope, a lifelong guide.

28. Happy Heart's Guide

In a world full of hustle and tides,
A happy heart gracefully glides.
Motivated by joy, each day anew,
Chasing dreams, skies ever blue.

Decisions they make, with clarity so clear,
Guided by joy, not by fear.
For happiness shines, like a guiding star,
Leading the way, making paths bright, no matter how far.

Loved by all, wherever they go,
Their cheerful spirit, always on show.
For a joyful heart, pure and true,

Draws love and warmth, like morning dew.

So be that ray, full of elation,
Spread your joy, without hesitation.
For a happy soul, in every situation,
Finds motivation, love, and inspiration.

29. The Digital Soul

In a world where wires intertwine with dreams,
Where consciousness flows like digital streams,
The Digital Soul, free from earthly hold,
Finds its home in the cloud, daring and bold.

No heartbeat, no breath, yet memories remain,
Life as data, an existence redefined and arcane.
Floating in bytes, in a vast sea of code,
Would we still feel, or would emotions erode?

Would love be a file, and tears just a glitch?
Would happiness be a switch, pain just a hitch?

The Digital Soul, in its vastness might soar,
But would it still cherish the human heart's core?

For in circuits and data, in the boundless web's fold,
There might still echo the tales our hearts once told.

30. Conversations with Shadows

My shadow and I, side by side we stand,
A fleeting shape on sunlit land.
"Who are you?" I ask, curious and keen,
A silent echo, both felt and seen.

"You're darkness in light," I note with a smile,
"But without the sun, you'd vanish awhile."
It dances and flits, a mirror of me,
A hint of what's hidden, of what one can't see.

I question its depth, its soft, silent play,
"Do you dream at night or fade away?"

It stretches and bends, neither solid nor air,
A companion so quiet, always there, yet rare.

Through laughter and tears, in sunshine and night,
My shadow holds secrets, both heavy and light.
Conversations profound, with this echo so slight,
My shadow and me, in the world's gentle light

31. Interstellar Heartbreak

A star and a planet, in the vast cosmic sea,
Danced close together, as close as can be.
The star, brightly shining, whispered a plea,
"Together forever, can't we just be?"

But orbits kept shifting, space vast and wide,
The planet kept drifting, despite how they tried.
Their love was a force, pulling them near,
Yet destiny's course was something to fear.

A moon gazed afar, at a comet's swift trail,
Hoping one day, her love wouldn't fail.
But comets keep moving, they don't stay in place,
Leaving the moon with just a brief trace.

In the vastness of space, where love stories unfold,
Celestial heartbreaks are tales often told.
For in cosmic dances, as stars gleam and chart,
Gravity pulls close, then tears them apart.

32. Silent Echoes

In the quiet corners of my mind, I hear,
Silent echoes, both distant and near.
Laughter long lost, in memories it stays,
Whispers of joy from forgotten days.

The murmur of home, where once I did roam,
Soft lullabies, in dreams they still come.
The rustle of leaves, from a tree now gone,
Yet in my heart, the breeze lingers on.

Footsteps that faded, voices that stilled,
In the silence, they're vividly filled.
Though the world outside remains quiet and still,
Silent echoes in memories thrill.

For sounds may vanish, but they never depart,
Living forever in the chambers of the heart.

33. The World in a Dewdrop

Upon a leaf, a dewdrop rests,
A tiny world, nature's bequest.
Inside its curve, reflections gleam,
Whole universes, or so it seems.

Majestic mountains, vast blue skies,
In that small sphere, magnified lies.
Creatures roam, too small to see,
Each droplet, a world's mystery.

Such wonder held in a space so slight,
Revealing secrets in the morning light.
In the tiniest corners, magic we find,
The world in a dewdrop, nature's remind

34. Tales of Forgotten Objects

In a drawer laid deep, a coin does sleep,
Tales of hands it knew, secrets it keeps.
Once it shined, in a spender's delight,
Now forgotten, lost from sight.

A button, once snug, on a coat so fine,
Now lies alone, no purpose to define.
It recalls the warmth, the laughter, the days,
When it held things close, in so many ways.

On a desk sits a pen, ink long dried,
Recalling the words, the tears, the pride.
Stories it penned, dreams it did trace,
Now silent, in this ever-spinning space.

Every object, though silent they stay,
Holds memories of a brighter day.
Tales of the past, in shadows they cast,
Whispering stories, of times that have passed.

35. Reverse Time

In a world flipped around, where time walks in reverse,
Goodbyes become hellos, and endings turn to firsts.
Babies grow to elders, then youthfully play,
Sunsets greet the morning, ending with the day.

Tears are wiped before they ever fall,
Laughter echoes, answering a distant call.
Lovers unmet, yet feelings stay strong,
Wondering if in reverse, did they truly belong?

Memories form before moments take place,
Chasing the origins of a familiar face.
In this backward dance, where past is the fore,
Love is rediscovered, loss is no more.

Yet even in reverse, one truth remains clear,
Emotions are timeless, always sincere.
Whether forwards or back, time's river may flow,
Hearts remember the love, and the warmth of its glow.

36. The Last Dream of the Night

At the edge where night kisses the dawn's first light,
Where dreams weave tales in a mystic flight,
There lies a vision, both vivid and profound,
The last enchanting whisper, before morning's sound.

Colors more vivid than the waking day's hue,
Scenarios impossible, yet they feel so true.
Flying fish, talking trees, rivers of gold,
Stories untold, in that dreamland bold.

Perhaps it's a whisper from a world afar,
Or a dance with memories, under a shooting star.
The clock's gentle tick, as reality nears,
Yet in that moment, the universe veers.

Then eyes slowly open, the dream starts to fade,
Leaving traces of wonder, of the adventures paraded.
The last dream of the night, profound and so clear,
A reminder of magic, always near.

37. Sentiments of Outer Space

In the vastness of dark, where no voices reside,
Space observes silently, with a cosmic pride.
It sees galaxies forming, a beautiful birth,
And watches their fading, returning to earth.

Stars glitter and gleam, then go supernova bright,
Space cradles their fire, in the deep of the night.
Feeling their warmth, their passion, their glow,
Witnessing stories only space could know.

Time moves differently here, both swift and slow,
As celestial bodies put on their grand show.
To space, they're but moments, fleeting and dear,
In an ever-expanding dance, year after year.

Oh, the sentiments of space, vast and profound,
Holding the mysteries of the universe unbound.
Watching, feeling, as stars come and go,
In the silent symphony of the cosmos' flow.

38. Odyssey of the Unknown

Curiosity, a spark, started out small,
In ancient caves, it began its call.
Wondering about fire, the stars, the sun,
It propelled mankind, a journey begun.

Through Egypt's sands, it questioned the Nile,
In Greece, it pondered existence awhile.
Rome's vast empire, with its might and lore,
Curiosity knocked on every door.

In Eastern lands, it sought wisdom's tree,
Mysteries of life, of what could be.
Through the dark ages, a guiding light,
Leading to the Renaissance, so bright.

Modern cities, to the digital age,
Curiosity penned every page.
From the atom's heart to the vast space beyond,
It's the quest that keeps us fond.

This odyssey of the unknown, forever to last,
Tied to the future, present, and past.
Curiosity, our guide, through thick and thin,
A timeless journey, that'll never end.

39. The Song of Silence

In the still of the night, silence sings its song,
Whispers of memories, where shadows belong.
No spoken word, yet tales it tells,
Of secret wishes, and magic spells.
The hush of a forest, before dawn's first light,
The quiet between heartbeats, soft and slight.
In the pause of a breath, or a gaze that lingers,
Silence tells stories, with invisible fingers.
Emotions it holds, both joy and despair,
The weight of a secret, the lightness of air.
In the gaps between words, where truth often lies,
Silence carries the answers, to our whys.
So, next time you find, a moment so still,
Listen to the silence, feel its gentle thrill.
For within its quiet, vast tales reside,
The song of silence, where truths often hide.

40. Ephemeral Moments

In whispers of a morning breeze,
A dewdrop clings to petals with ease.
Sunrise paints the sky's canvas gold,
A moment's magic, a sight to behold.

Unnoticed gems on blades of green,
Sparkling diamonds in dawn's serene.
Footprints on sandy shores fade away,
Ephemeral tales that waves convey.

Children's laughter in the park's sweet sound,
Brief as shooting stars, dancing around.
Butterflies with colours so bright,
Fleeting beauty, a graceful flight.

A touch, a glance, a knowing smile,
Moments that make life worthwhile.
Each second's gift, a story to tell,
Ephemeral treasures, in our hearts swell.

41. The Weather Report of the Soul

A sunny smile, a thunderous frown,
In weathered hearts, emotions are found,
Love's warm breeze, despair's cold hail,
Every feeling tells its tale.

Clouds of worry, winds of delight,
A tempest of anger takes its flight,
Mist of mystery, fog of doubt,
Emotions twist, spin, and spout.

Rain of tears, a storm of grief,
Weathered hearts seek relief,
Snow of purity, ice of disdain,
In weather's grasp, feelings remain.

A hurricane of passion, a drizzle of sadness,
A gust of surprise, a whirlwind of madness,
Every emotion, a weather's grasp,
In the climate of life, they take their place.

Tornado of turmoil, a gentle breeze of trust,
In weather's patterns, emotions adjust,
From calm to storm, from drizzle to pour,
Feelings ebb and flow, forevermore.

Sunrise of hope, sunset of sorrow,
Weathered emotions, today and tomorrow,
In skies and seasons, feelings intertwine,
A meteorological dance, complex and divine.

Grasp the weather, feel its grace,
In every emotion, find your place,
For weathered hearts know the way,
To love and feel, every single day.

42. Ink and Emotions: Sketches of Life

Cubist love, Surrealist dream,
Emotions painted, a creative scheme,
Feelings in colour, shapes, and line,
A canvas of heart, so fine.

Impressionist joy, Abstract dismay,
Each stroke and hue conveys a way,
Of feeling, seeing, understanding deep,
In art's touch, emotions leap.

Gothic fear, Romantic bliss,
Artistic movements paint feelings like this,
Expressionist anger, Minimalist peace,
In every style, emotions never cease.

Renaissance respect, Pop Art surprise,
Emotions rendered under artistic skies,
Baroque complexity, Futurism's speed,
In every brushstroke, emotions take heed.

Mural of melancholy, sculpture of pride,
In galleries of heart, emotions reside,
A palette of passions, a texture of tears,
Artistic emotions, yearning through years.

Dada's confusion, Fauvism's flame,
Emotions and art, never quite the same,
Each movement a mood, each style a state,
In the artwork of feelings, love and hate.

Paint your emotions, sculpt your dreams,
In art's wide spectrum, everything gleams,
With colours and shapes, lines and design,
Your feelings are art, uniquely divine.

From canvas to sculpture, from oil to ink,
Emotions are art, a creative link,
So paint your love, sketch your fears,
For art's the language that everyone hears.

Dada: Dada was an avant-garde art movement that emerged during World War I. It was characterized by its rejection of traditional artistic values and its acceptance of chaos, absurdity, and anti-establishment sentiments. "Dada's confusion" implies the unconventional and often perplexing nature of Dada art, which aimed to challenge and disrupt societal norms.

Fauvism: Fauvism was an early 20th-century art movement known for its vibrant and bold use of colour. "Fauvism's flame" represents the intense and fiery colours used by Fauvist artists to convey emotions and create visual impact. Fauvism celebrated vivid colour and distortion for emotional expression.

43. Synesthetic Love: Feelings in Colours and Sounds

What colour is jealousy? A greenish haze,
What does happiness taste like? Sweet sunny days,
Anger's a red flash, love's a soft touch,
In this blending of feelings, senses mean so much.

What sound is sorrow? A low mournful cry,
What scent is excitement? Fresh breeze in the sky,
Fear's a dark shadow, trust's a warm glow,
Emotions and senses in a vivid flow.

What flavour is kindness? A comforting meal,
What texture is anxiety? A nervous unreal,
The melody of friendship, the hue of despair,
In this symphony of senses, feelings are there.

What rhythm is courage? A strong steady beat,
What fragrance is longing? A memory so sweet,
The taste of forgiveness, the colour of grace,
In every sensation, emotions connect in place.

So see with your heart, and feel with your eyes,
Taste with your thoughts, hear with surprise,
In this sensory world, senses entwine,
A colourful, flavourful, emotional rhyme.

Explore your emotions, through sight, taste, and sound,
In this landscape of feelings, wonders are found,
A unique way to feel, to understand, to see,
Synesthetic senses, a sensory spree.

44. A Mythology of Emotions: Gods, Monsters, and Heroes

In a world where feelings take form,
Myths and legends are the norm,
Each emotion, a deity or beast,
In this fantastical world, to say the least.

Love's a goddess, gentle and fair,
With a touch of grace in her golden hair,
Courage, a hero, strong and bold,
His story of bravery often told.

Fear's a shadowy monster that lurks,
In dark corners where anxiety works,
Joy's a sprite, dancing in light,
Spreading happiness, pure delight.

Anger's a dragon, fiery and red,
Its flames of fury widely spread,
Sorrow's a siren, singing her song,
A melody for those who feel they don't belong.

Hope's a phoenix, rising anew,
From ashes of despair, it breaks through,

Jealousy's a goblin, green and sly,
Its envious gaze never passing by.

Trust's a wise old wizard with a staff,
Guiding hearts along life's path,
Excitement's a unicorn, rare and wild,
A creature of wonder for every child.

In this world of myth and lore,
Emotions are beings never seen before,
Gods, monsters, heroes abide,
In the landscape where feelings reside.

So imagine a world, fantastical and grand,
Where emotions live, not just in the land,
A mythology of feelings, unique and divine,
In every heart, in yours and mine.

45. Reflections in the Roaring Sea

Upon the shore, I stand in awe,
High sea tides rise, with no flaw,
A dance of nature, wild and free,
A reflection of my heart, turbulent as the sea.

The waves crash with ferocious might,
Echoing my soul's ceaseless fight,
Each crest and trough, a thought profound,
A rhythm in chaos, yet harmony found.

Turbulence within, a stormy sea,
Mimics the waves that crash before me,
In roaring tides, my soul laid bare,
A constant battle, wear and tear.

A pull, a tug, emotions surge,
Like tides commanded by the moon's urge,
With every swell, my thoughts combine,
In endless waves, both yours and mine.

Yet in this turmoil, beauty resides,
A lesson learned from nature's strides,
Hold the storm, the wild sea's art,
Find strength and peace in a turbulent heart.

For high sea tides, with power and grace,

Remind me of life's unyielding pace,

A force untamed, a love so deep,

A mirror to my soul, the thoughts I weave.

46. The River and Mountain Within: Achieving the Impossible

In lands where mighty mountains rise,
And rivers flow with grace and might,
I find a path, a vision clear,
A journey through both day and night.

With peaks that touch the sky above,
Mountains bold, a challenge faced,
I see my goals, those towering heights,
With positivity encased.

The climb is steep, the path is rough,
Yet step by step, I find my way,
With motivation as my guide,
I conquer fears, come what may.

The river's course, a winding path,
Through valleys low and canyons deep,
It carves its way with patient force,
A lesson learned that I shall keep.

For I'm the river, strong and true,
And I'm the mountain, tall and grand,

With determination in my soul,
I reach for dreams, take my stand.

I face the climb, accept the fall,
With courage, strength, and endless drive,
I know that I can reach the top,
With heart and mind, I'll thrive, I'll strive.

For mountains high and rivers wild,
Are but reflections of my quest,
A symbol of my boundless will,
A life accepted, a soul at rest.

I'll forge ahead, I'll never yield,
With love and passion, I'll succeed,
The mountains call, the rivers sing,
I can achieve, I'll take the lead.

In nature's wisdom, truth resides,
With positivity and grace,
I'll conquer all, I'll rise above,
I'll win this lifelong, wondrous race.

47. Classrooms and Kitchens: The Legacy of a Loving Mom

In halls of learning, classrooms bright,
A mother toiled from morn till night,
With eyes aglow and heart so true,
She shaped the minds, her love she knew.

A teacher's grace, a mother's touch,
She gave to us, she gave so much,
Despite the struggles, the weight she bore,
She raised us high, so much she swore.

With hands so worn, yet smile so wide,
She hid the tears, the times she cried,
A warrior's spirit, strong and brave,
For us, her children, she'd always save.

We wondered how, we wondered why,
She managed all, with no sign or sigh,
Of weakness, pain, or sorrow's hold,
Her love for us, a story bold.

But now we see, we understand,
The hidden trials, life's complex strand,
The weary nights, the silent pleas,
Her sacrifice, her wish to ease.

For in her eyes, we were her sun,
Her joy, her pride, the cherished ones,
She masked her pain, her struggle keen,
To give us dreams, a life serene.

Oh, love you, Mom, with all our hearts,
For all you've done, the endless parts,
You've played in life, with grace and cheer,
A mother's love, forever dear.

Your story's etched in time and space,
A tale of strength, of endless grace,
We honour you, we hold you near,
A mother's love, no bounds, no peer.

48. Digital Chains: A Youth's Call to the Real World

In chambers dim, where screens aglow,
A world of web, a virtual show,
The youth entwined in cyberspace,
Lost in the glow, a distant place.

A generation once so free,
Now captive to technology,
Their faces lit, yet eyes so dim,
A loneliness begins to skim.

They wander through the online maze,
In search of likes, a fleeting gaze,
But what they find is emptiness,
A void that's filled with cold duress.

But listen now, young hearts and minds,
A world awaits, a life that binds,
Beyond the screen, beyond the chat,
A life of meaning, pure and intact.

Look up and see the sky so wide,
The stars, the sun, don't let them hide,
Feel the grass beneath your feet,
Hear the birds, their songs so sweet.

Reconnect with friends, with laughter true,
Discover the world, it waits for you,
Find hobbies, passions, love's warm glow,
Leave behind the screen's cold, empty show.

For in the world, with all its might,
Exists a path, a life so bright,
With human touch and nature's grace,
A warmth, a glow, a real welcome.

So break the chains, escape the web,
Live life anew, don't let it ebb,
The world is vast, with much to see,
Discover it now, be bold, be free.

You'll find a joy, a peace within,
A life connected, a genuine win,
Your heart will soar, your soul ignite,
A life more active, more pure, more bright

49. Gold and Family: A Maid's Perspective

In gilded halls and rooms pristine,
She moves with grace, yet seldom seen,
A maid whose heart is far away,
In thoughts of home, where children play.

Her hands, they clean; her eyes, they gleam,
With dreams of love and life's sweet theme,
Her husband's face, her children's cheer,
These simple joys she holds so dear.

She sees the wealth, the lavish fare,
The luxuries beyond compare,
Yet never does her heart give in,
To envy's call or longing's sin.

For she's a mother, strong and true,
A wife whose love will not undo,
Her soul is bound to hearth and home,
No matter where her feet may roam.

At night, she leaves the mansion grand,
Returns to life's more humble stand,
Her children's hugs, her husband's kiss,

These are her wealth, her endless bliss.

She's more than just a servant's face,
She's human, full of dignity and grace,
Her feelings deep, her love profound,
In simple joys, her truth is found.

Her wealth lies not in gold or fame,
But in her family's loving claim,
A maid, a mother, strong and true,
A human, just like me and you.

50. Barbarism Reborn: A Modern Reflection

Long ago, when fires were big,
And people fought without a twig,
Strength ruled, and wildness was the way,
It seemed barbaric every day.

They used swords, clubs, and sharp spears,
Yelling loudly, spreading fears,
A time of wild and strong desire,
When people lived with so much fire.

But look now, what can you see?
A world that's changed, but not fully,
People are cold, hiding their mark,
With hidden knives, and words that bark.

We don't use blades, but words that sting,
Lies and smiles are the new thing,
We fight with words, not with swords,
But we're still playing the same old chords.

The wild urge is still around,
In work, in politics, it's found,
Our weapons now are words, so sly,
A new way to fight, but the same old why.

We don't use swords, but words that cut,
We fight online, but the doors aren't shut,
We talk of growth, of things so new,
But the wild ways are still in view.

Have we changed? What's the cost?
In this new world, what have we lost?
We act so new, but we're still the same,
Just new rules in an old, old game.

A look in the mirror, a hard, hard stare,
Shows we're still wild, and we still care,
Wild back then, wild right now,
Just new ways, but the same somehow.

51. The Way of Karma

Avoid the path where shadows loom,
The karmas dark, they call our doom,
They linger on in mystery,
And shape our life's unfolding history.

In lives before, the seeds were sown,
The karmas cast, the future known,
The deeds of then shape what we are,
Each action, a guiding mark.

A lie once told, a trust once broke,
Resonates beyond words spoke,
Its ripple felt in hearts and minds,
A karmic debt that's not confined.

The anger's burst, the envy's sting,
These petty acts their karma bring,
A cycle woven from life to life,
A tangled web of pain and strife.

A greed that grips, a pride that soars,
They close our hearts and lock our doors,
These karmas wrong, they shade our soul,
They burden us, exact their toll.

Accept the wisdom, clear the slate,
It's never early, never late,
Transform the karmas, make them right,
A life renewed in love's pure light.

Acknowledgements

Writing this book has been a journey that couldn't have been completed without the unwavering support and love of a number of incredible people.

Firstly, to my pillars of strength, my mom and dad, whose love and wisdom have shaped me into who I am today. Your sacrifices and encouragement have always motivated me to aim higher.

To my loving wife, Pooja, you've been my rock and my muse. Your love has inspired countless lines and verses in this book, and for that, I'm eternally grateful.

To my son Pranav, whose honesty serves as a constant reminder of the purest form of expression, and my daughter Aaritra, who bursts with energy and lights up my world—thank you for being the joy of my life.

Special thanks go to Nilu, who has lent her artistic touch to this book with beautiful illustrations that bring my words to life.

Lastly, my biggest inspirations have often come from the quiet moments spent on my balcony, gazing at trees, birds, the sky, nature's different moods, the rain, airplanes, and the sun and moon in their celestial dance. These elements have been the silent fuel to my poetic fire.

Thank you all for being a part of this incredible journey. Your impact has been indelible, and this book is as much yours as it is mine.

Bhannu Arora is an author whose writings resonate across various themes and emotions. In 2017, he penned "10 Essentials to the Blueprint of Happiness," a self-help book aimed at guiding readers toward personal joy and contentment.

His 2022 release, "She- The Shimla Diaries," is a narrative poetry collection that tells the poignant story of a teenage girl working as a maid in a British officer's house in Shimla, the summer capital of pre-independent India. The beautiful verses transports readers to a historical era, offering a glimpse into the girl's life and the complexities of the time.

Bhannu's latest work, "INK AND EMOTIONS," delves into various emotional challenges of life. With his profound understanding of human emotions, he explores themes that resonate with many, providing solace and insight.

An ex- banker, Bhannu is a numerologist, vastu expert and an angelic healer.

INK and EMOTIONS" is a collection of 51 poems that take you on a journey through the human heart. Exploring feelings like anger, love, despair, and triumph, each verse unlocks a new layer of understanding. Whether you want to explore whispers of the divine or face modern challenges like bullying, this book offers a unique window into diverse experiences and emotions.

Open these pages, and you'll find worlds within words, from seeing the entire world in a dewdrop to hearing the profound song of silence. More than just poetry, "INK and EMOTIONS" is a heartfelt invitation to feel, think, and live more deeply. It's a vibrant exploration of life in all its raw and beautiful forms, waiting to be discovered.